Reading
Imagine

LEVEL 1

Animals 1, 2, 3!

Sylvia Sikundar
Series Editor – Jean Conteh

MACMILLAN

About this Book

To the Teacher or Parent

This is a counting book. It begins with some simple pages to help young children learn to count to ten with pictures of animals. Then, it has some more pages with humorous pictures to give children more practice in counting in an amusing way.

The book will help to develop young children's interest and enjoyment in reading. You can use it in different ways to teach young children who are just beginning to learn to read. It can also help older children, who can read a little, to become better readers.

You, or an older child, could share the book with younger children.

- Begin by talking with the children about the pictures on the cover. Ask them to tell you what they can see.
- Go through the book page by page, talking about the pictures. Ask the children to name what they can see in the pictures.
- Then, go through pages 3–11 with the children and see if they can identify the numerals on each page.
- See if they can count the items in the pictures, and also count the butterflies, which appear on each page.
- Read the words aloud. Let them join in or repeat after you.
- Practise the words with the children, e.g. ask them to point to individual words as you say them.
- Pages 12 and 13 will help you to review the counting and also the names of the animals.
- Then, pages 14–24 give more practice in counting. There are many different things to count in the pictures. See what you can find!

Older children may be able to read the sentences for themselves while you listen. Use every opportunity to help them identify things they know, to learn the names of new things, and to count the things they see in the pictures.

Above all, help the children to enjoy this book – this is the best way to make them interested to learn more and to become independent readers.

1

One elephant,

2

two zebras,

3

three hippos,

four giraffes,

5

five frogs,

6

six goats,

seven spiders,

8

eight donkeys,

nine crocodiles,

10

ten monkeys.

One elephant

Two zebras

Three hippos

Four giraffes

Five frogs

Six goats

Seven spiders

Eight donkeys

Nine crocodiles

Ten monkeys

1 2 3 4

5 6 7 8 9 10

1

One elephant chases a mouse.

Two zebras paint a house.

Three hippos drink some tea.

4

Four giraffes on the sea.

5

Five frogs drive new cars.

Six goats count the stars.

7

Seven spiders walk to town.

Eight donkeys jump up and down.

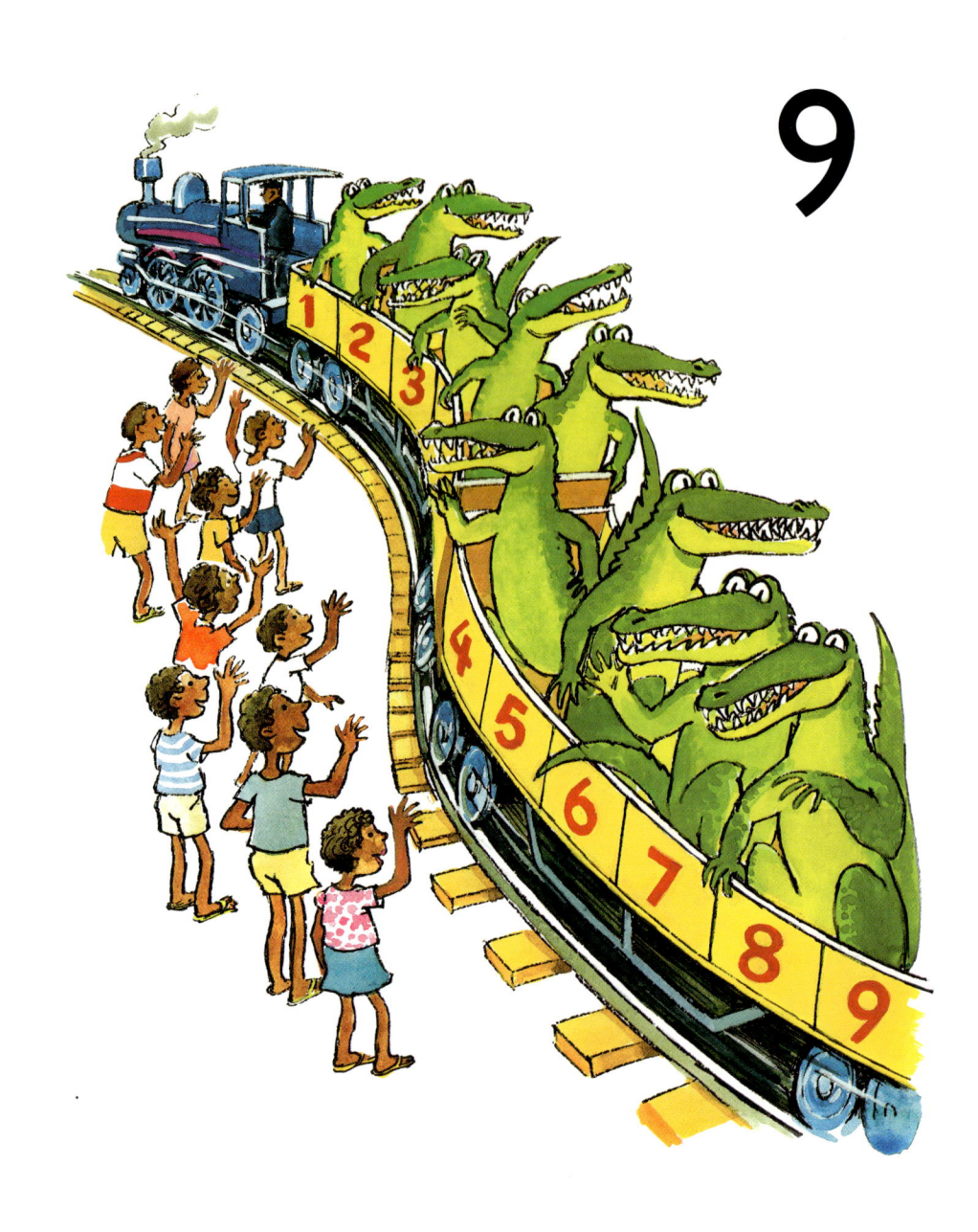

Nine crocodiles on the train.

Ten monkeys in the rain.

Activity page

1 Where are the butterflies?

2 How many animals can you find?

24